Bears, Cannons, Blood and Why Shakespeare's Theatre was Best

written by Catherine Allison
illustrated by Kathy Baxendale and Nick Schon

Contents

Was Shakespeare's theatre the best?	2
Going to the theatre was a great day out	4
There were different types of theatre to choose from	6
Theatre-going was great value for money	8
The audience were part of the action	10
The plays had exciting stories	12
There was a different play to see every other day!	14
There was never a dull moment on stage	16
The plays were easy to understand	18
The theatres were so well designed	20
The special effects were so realistic!	22
The theatre was where people could hear beautiful poetry	24
The actors were very talented	26
Summary	30
Glossary	31
Index	32

Introduction: Was Shakespeare's theatre the best?

These are some of the views that people today have about the plays of William Shakespeare and the theatre of his time.

> The language is so old-fashioned. No one really spoke like that!

> There wasn't any scenery, was there? Plays must have been very dull to watch!

> The plays are boring! Nothing ever happens!

> Why should I want to learn about Shakespeare when he lived hundreds of years ago?

You may agree with some (or all) of them yourself. But did you know that if you had gone to the theatre in Shakespeare's day you could have seen:

- real cannons firing
- dancing and singing
- expert sword fighting
- fancy costumes
- great stories (better than any television soap opera today!)
- heroes, villains and clowns
- ghosts
- witches chanting spells
- boys dressed as girls pretending to be boys, and
- statues coming to life?

There were lots of other reasons why it was great fun being part of a theatre audience 500 years ago …

Going to the theatre was a great day out

In England in the 1500s, going to the theatre was one of the most popular entertainments. Most people couldn't read, and there was no television or cinema, so if they wanted to listen to a story, they went to the theatre.

Even the journey to the theatre was exciting. Theatres were round or octagonal so they were very unusual-looking buildings. On days when a play was being performed, a flag would be raised above the theatre so that people could see it from miles around. In smaller towns, the actors would parade through the streets to advertise the day's show.

Several London theatres, like the Globe Theatre where many of Shakespeare's plays were performed, were on the south side of the River Thames, at a distance from the city centre. Rich people paid to be rowed across the river in boats, while working people walked across London Bridge in crowds. Just before a play began, a trumpet would sound to tell the audience to hurry to the theatre.

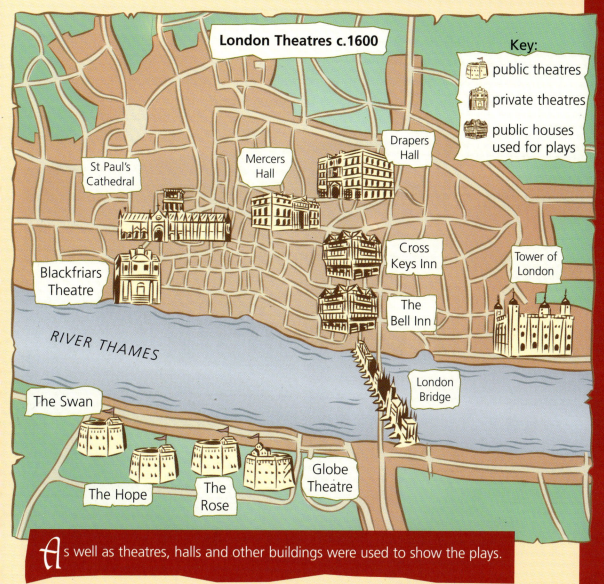

As well as theatres, halls and other buildings were used to show the plays.

There was a **playhouse** of some kind within two miles of every Londoner.

There were different types of theatre to choose from

There were two types of theatre in Shakespeare's day.

Public theatres were cheap, noisy and packed with people, and the plays performed there were often full of action and comedy. Several plays were performed every week, so you could choose a play to suit your mood.

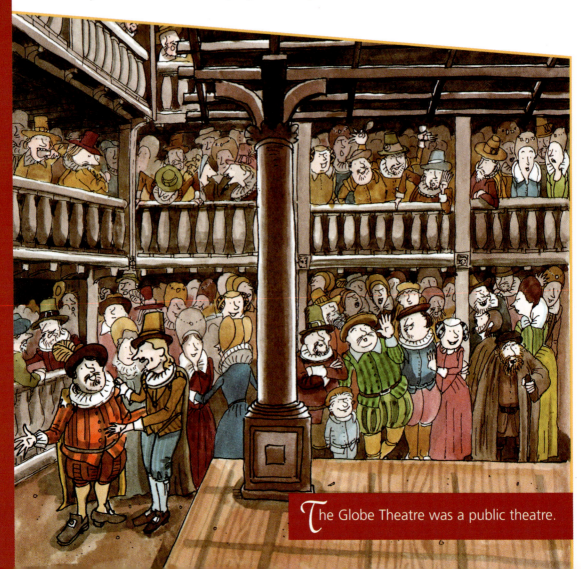

The Globe Theatre was a public theatre.

If you wanted to go to a smaller theatre, with fewer people and more comfortable seats, you went to one of the private theatres. Shakespeare's acting company performed the same plays at both types of theatre, but some **playwrights** refused to have their plays performed on the public stages because they thought the audiences didn't listen properly!

Blackfriars Theatre was a private theatre which attracted a more select audience.

You could go to see plays performed by adult actors, but there were also acting companies where all the actors were young boys. Some people thought that the boy companies were better than the adult companies.

Theatre-going was great value for money

In the public theatres, you could see a play of two hours or more, for as little as 1d (less than one penny) followed by music and dancing.

galleries

groundlings

yard

With a 1d ticket you had to stand up in the **yard** in front of the stage. But that was a good place to be because it was very close to the actors. The people in the audience who stood in the yard were known as "**groundlings**".

A seat in one of the galleries round the sides of the theatre cost 2d. You could hire a cushion to sit on to make the seat more comfortable.

The richest people paid 6d to sit in a box (called the "lord's room") above the stage. Sitting there you had an excellent view of the stage, and the rest of the audience could see you in all your fine clothes, too.

The audience were part of the action

In Shakespeare's day, theatre was an interactive experience! The audience, especially the groundlings, talked all the time. Sometimes they discussed what was happening on stage, but not always. When they enjoyed an actor's speech or one of the special effects on stage, they clapped and cheered loudly. If they found a play boring, they shouted and complained. Food, like apples, pears and nuts, was on sale in the theatres. If the audience got bored, they would throw their food at the actors. (Plays were always performed in daylight, so it was easier to hit the actors!)

It must have been difficult for the actors to concentrate or make themselves heard over the noise, but at least they could always tell if the audience were enjoying themselves! And they sometimes changed parts of their speeches from one day to the next so that audiences would enjoy them more.

The plays had exciting stories

Plays in Shakespeare's time had everything that soap operas have today: family arguments and broken friendships, love, jealousy, hatred, violence and mystery.

Hamlet
by W. Shakespeare

Do you believe in ghosts?

... Hamlet, the prince of Denmark, misses his dead father the king and thinks about him all the time. One night, his friends are terrified when they see the ghost of Hamlet's father walking on the battlements of the castle, dressed in his armour as if ready for battle. It seems that the ghost has a message for his son. At first, Hamlet cannot believe his friends' story, but the following night he decides to see if the ghost will appear and speak to him ...

starring Richard Burbage

Romeo and Juliet
by W. Shakespeare

A pair of star-crossed lovers

The tragic story of Romeo and Juliet, two teenagers in love whose families hate each other and forbid the lovers to meet. But the lovers will not be kept apart. They meet on the balcony to Juliet's bedroom one night, and swear their undying love for each other. But tragically their plans to be together go wrong. Juliet's parents try to force her to marry another boy, so she takes a sleeping potion and pretends that she is dead. Romeo finds her asleep and thinks she is really dead, and kills himself. At that very moment, the sleeping potion begins to wear off, and Juliet wakes up ...

starring Edward Alleyn

There was a different play to see every other day!

Comedy – A Midsummer Night's Dream

History – Henry V

Each theatre wanted to attract the biggest audience. Some theatres would put on as many as six different plays a week to get the audiences to come. Playwrights could tell which stories were the most popular with audiences by counting the number of apple cores thrown at the actors at the end of a show!

The main types of play on offer were:

- Comedies – lighthearted stories with happy endings
- Histories – stories about people from the past, often kings and queens. The history of England was particularly popular, especially stories of war and victory for English armies
- Tragedies – stories about rich or powerful people, often kings or noblemen, who are doomed to fail in life

The old stories are the best

Quite often, the audience already knew the story of a play when they went to the theatre. They might have seen it on stage before, or sometimes it was a traditional story that parents had told their children down through the generations. People enjoyed seeing a well-loved story performed in a big theatre.

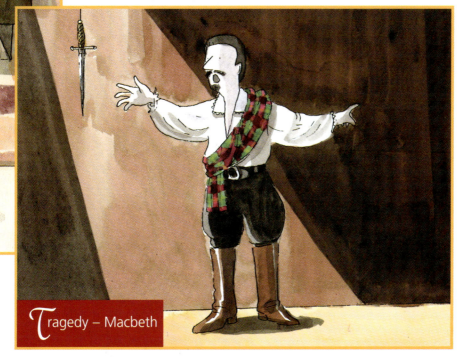

Tragedy – Macbeth

There was never a dull moment on stage

Shakespeare wrote comedies, histories and tragedies. He was an actor as well as a playwright, so he knew how audiences complained if the play was boring. Audiences loved dramatic stories about wars and battles, mysteries to be solved, magical happenings, or characters in disguises. Shakespeare's plays gave them all these things, with dazzling costumes, music and special effects.

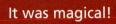

The Winter's Tale

The most amazing moment for me was when the statue of Hermione, the wife of the King of Sicilia, seemed to come to life. The statue did look very life-like, but it was standing there so still in the centre of the stage, I never expected anything to happen. It was right at the end of the play, and the king had just met his long-lost daughter. Then the statue moved, and beautiful Hermione was alive again. It was magical!

Olivia falls in love with Viola when she is dressed as a boy.

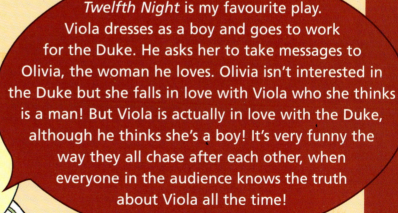

Twelfth Night is my favourite play. Viola dresses as a boy and goes to work for the Duke. He asks her to take messages to Olivia, the woman he loves. Olivia isn't interested in the Duke but she falls in love with Viola who she thinks is a man! But Viola is actually in love with the Duke, although he thinks she's a boy! It's very funny the way they all chase after each other, when everyone in the audience knows the truth about Viola all the time!

The plays were easy to understand

In Shakespeare's day, the stage could become a ship on a stormy sea, the court of a powerful foreign king, the centre of Ancient Rome or a leafy forest in England – with just the words of the actors, a few **props**, and a change of costume. The audience used their imagination to provide the other details.

Often the plays started with a **prologue** which told the audience where and when the play was set. When the setting changed, a character spoke to the audience and explained where the scene was taking place. There was no scenery to change, so plays moved fast, from one time in history to another, or one country to another, without any break in the action.

Actors also used props to show that the setting had changed. If there was a throne on the stage, the audience knew that the new scene was set in a royal palace. If an actor came on stage carrying a bow and arrows, the audience would know that he was going hunting. If a painting of the moon appeared, the scene was taking place at night.

Simple country clothes told the audience that the scene had a country setting, while richly embroidered clothes meant the setting was a royal palace or a rich person's home.

This scene from Hamlet takes place in a graveyard. The trapdoor in the stage is used as a grave. Together with the words the actors speak, this is enough to help the audience imagine a real graveyard setting.

The theatres were so well designed

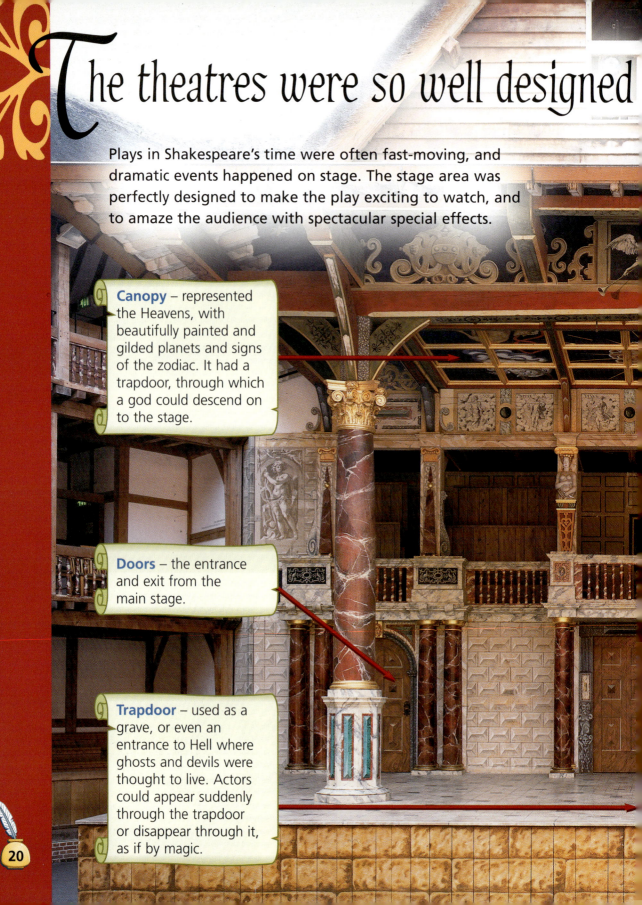

Plays in Shakespeare's time were often fast-moving, and dramatic events happened on stage. The stage area was perfectly designed to make the play exciting to watch, and to amaze the audience with spectacular special effects.

Canopy – represented the Heavens, with beautifully painted and gilded planets and signs of the zodiac. It had a trapdoor, through which a god could descend on to the stage.

Doors – the entrance and exit from the main stage.

Trapdoor – used as a grave, or even an entrance to Hell where ghosts and devils were thought to live. Actors could appear suddenly through the trapdoor or disappear through it, as if by magic.

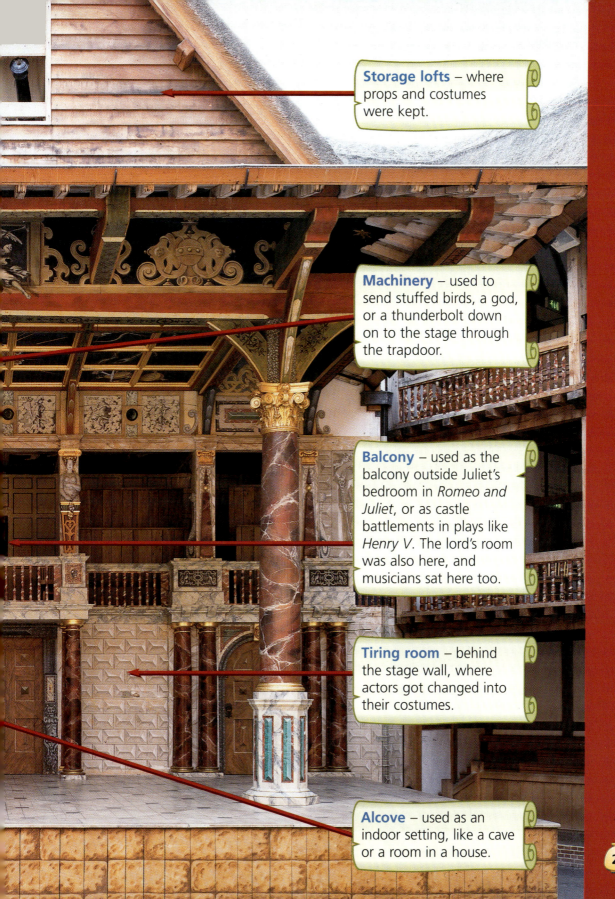

Storage lofts – where props and costumes were kept.

Machinery – used to send stuffed birds, a god, or a thunderbolt down on to the stage through the trapdoor.

Balcony – used as the balcony outside Juliet's bedroom in *Romeo and Juliet*, or as castle battlements in plays like *Henry V*. The lord's room was also here, and musicians sat here too.

Tiring room – behind the stage wall, where actors got changed into their costumes.

Alcove – used as an indoor setting, like a cave or a room in a house.

The special effects were so realistic!

Cannons

What could be more exciting in a battle scene than real cannons firing real cannon balls – the flash of light, the tremendous noise and the smell of gunpowder? Cannons were fired regularly from the roofs of the London theatres during Shakespeare's time without any problems. Then in 1613, during a performance of the play *Henry VIII*, a cannon was fired, the theatre's thatched roof caught fire, and in two hours the whole Globe Theatre had burnt to the ground.

Blood

When an actor was stabbed with a sword during a stage fight, he bled real blood! He hid a sponge soaked in animal blood under his shirt, and when the sword tip touched the sponge, the blood came out.

Storms

The theatres used **thundersheets** to make storm noises. Sometimes cannon balls were rolled from side to side to make the right kind of sound.

Bears

There may even have been live brown bears on stage in Shakespeare's time! There were **bear gardens** in London, so these dangerous wild animals were certainly not far away from Shakespeare's theatre, the Globe. Shakespeare's *The Winter's Tale* features the stage direction "Exit pursued by a bear". Some people think that perhaps a real bear was brought on stage during the play at this point!

The theatre was where people could hear beautiful poetry

Some of the best poetry in the English language comes from the plays of Shakespeare and his fellow playwrights. Shakespeare chose beautiful words and rhythms for his poetry to make the audience imagine the English countryside.

> I know a bank where the wild thyme blows,
> Where oxlips and the nodding violet grows,
> Quite **over-canopied** with **luscious** woodbine,
> With sweet musk-roses, and with eglantine.
>
> *A Midsummer Night's Dream*

over-canopied overhung
luscious sweet-smelling

He could make the audience imagine how it would feel before a terrible battle.

> ... when the blast of war blows in our ears,
> Then imitate the action of the tiger;
> Stiffen the **sinews**, summon up the blood,
> Disguise fair nature with **hard-favour'd rage;**
>
> *Henry V*

And remember, Shakespeare used the language that people spoke in his day, so the audience would have had no trouble understanding it.

sinews   muscle power
hard-favour'd rage   unaccustomed anger

The actors were very talented

Imagine seeing your favourite actors on stage, so close to you that you could look them right in the eye! At theatres like the Globe, you could do this every day of the week. From the 1580s onwards people began to go to plays to see star actors, just as people do with films today.

A poster for a modern film adaptation of one of Shakespeare's plays.

Nowadays, people go to the cinema to see famous actors. This poster shows Leonardo di Caprio as Romeo in a modern film adaptation of Romeo and Juliet.

Richard Burbage was a star actor. Shakespeare wrote the parts of Hamlet, Othello and King Lear for him. When he acted the death of Hamlet the audience and the other actors thought that he was really dying!

Burbage was an actor who also built the Globe Theatre in 1599.

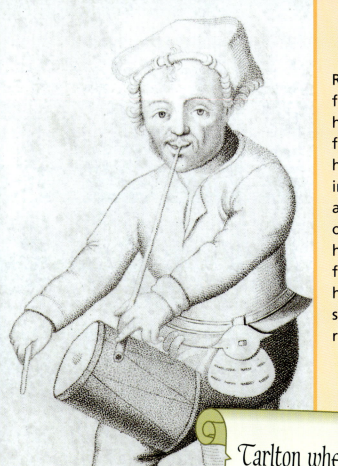

Richard Tarlton.

Richard Tarlton was the most famous and popular clown of his time. He was best known for **slapstick** comedy, and for his jokes which were published in a book after he died. He was always introduced by a tune on the pipe and **tabor**, and he was so funny that even his face peeping through the hangings at the back of the stage could make audiences roar with laughter.

Tarlton when his head was onely seene,
The **tirehouse** dore and **tapisterie** betweene
Set all the **multitude** in such a laughter,
They could not **hold** for scarse an houre after.

tirehouse   dressing room
tapisterie   curtain
multitude   audience
hold   stop

Actors were very good at what they did – they had to be or the audience would throw food at them! They had tremendous memories. They learned their lines by heart, and a leading role might be over 800 lines long.

They needed to project their voices over the noise of the audience. They also needed to change their voices to fit the different characters they played.

They had other talents as well.

☞ Many plays contained fight scenes, or battles. People were used to seeing prize fights on stage, so actors had to be expert fighters if they were to convince the audience. In sword fights the actors used real swords, so any mistake could be fatal. They also had to learn how to fall without hurting themselves or tearing their costumes.

☛ Some plays, especially the comedies, needed actors who could sing and play instruments.

☛ Actors needed to be able to dance in different styles, from country dancing to elegant court dancing.

☛ There were no female actors on stage until 1660. All female roles were played by young boy actors. As well as learning to speak like women, they also had to learn to move in feminine ways.

Summary

So, do you think you would have enjoyed going to the theatre in Shakespeare's time?

- You could have chatted to all your friends, eaten snacks and told the actors what you thought of them.

- You could have laughed at the clowns, cried with the victims and hissed at the villains.

- You could have seen the most spectacular special effects.

- You could have heard the most beautiful poetry, written by the greatest playwright of all time.

What more could you want for one penny?

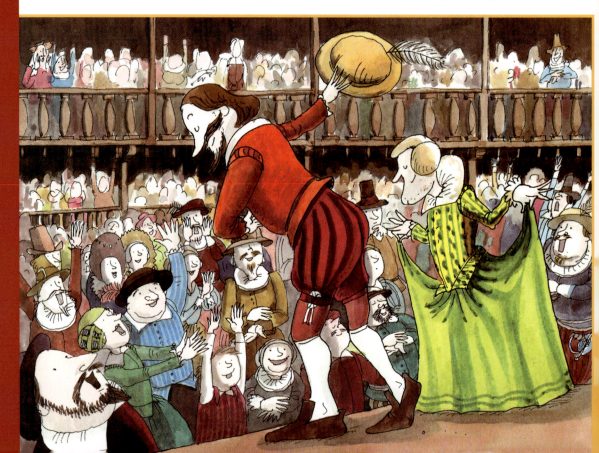

Glossary

bear garden   a place where bears were put on show to the public or used for bearbaiting

groundling   a member of the audience who stood in the yard

playhouse   a theatre

playwright   someone who writes plays

prologue   an introduction spoken by the narrator

props   movable objects used to make a play more realistic

slapstick   humour with lots of visual and physical jokes, like people getting wet or falling over

tabor   a small drum

thundersheet   a large tin sheet shaken to make storm noises

yard   the area in front of the stage where the audience stood

Shakespeare's theatre was the best!

Index

action 6, 28–29
actors 7, 10, 26–29
advertising 4
audience 7, 10–11

bears 23
Blackfriars Theatre 7
blood 22
boys 7, 29
Burbage, Richard 27

cannons 22
comedy 6, 15, 26
costumes 18–19

entertainment 4

ghosts 12
Globe Theatre 4–6, 22, 27
groundlings 8, 10

Hamlet 12
histories 15

language 24–25
London 5

plays 2–3, 18–19
   choice of 6, 14
   Shakespeare's 12–13, 16–17
   stories 12–15
   types of 15

poetry 24–25
prices 8–9
private theatres 7
props 18–19
public theatres 6

Romeo and Juliet 13

scenery 18
seats 7, 9
Shakespeare
   plays 12–13, 16–17
   poetry 24–25
special effects 22–23
stories 12–15
storms 23

Tarlton, Richard 26
theatres
   parts of 8–9, 20–21
   types of 6–7
tickets 8–9
tragedies 15
trumpets 5
Twelfth Night 16

The Winter's Tale 17
women actors 29